Sand to Stone and Back Again

Nancy Bo Flood

PHOTOGRAPHS BY

Tony Kuyper

FULCRUM
GOLDEN, COLORADO

To my grains of sand—
Megan, Michael, Elizabeth, and Macey…
diamonds of joy, you are.
—Nancy Bo Flood

For Andy, who introduced me to the darkroom,
and for Guy, who showed me how to see the light.
—Tony Kuyper

Changing man thought he would never change.
He would be the same forever
Like a rock at the edge of time.

I am a goblin hiding in moon shadows.

Or a hoodoo

standing atop a white shale shelf.

In Monument Valley,

look for me in giant mittens.

A full moon peeks in between.

I am sandstone.

I am always changing,

just like you.

Sometimes

I am a mesa,

or a narrow,

winding canyon.

Sometimes

I am a desert,

a soft dune resting,

or a tough old butte.

I shelter deer, pack rats, antelope, and bats.

And hikers, like you, or long ago, the Ancient Ones.

In my canyons they built their homes,

painted pictures,

carved messages,

and left handprints.

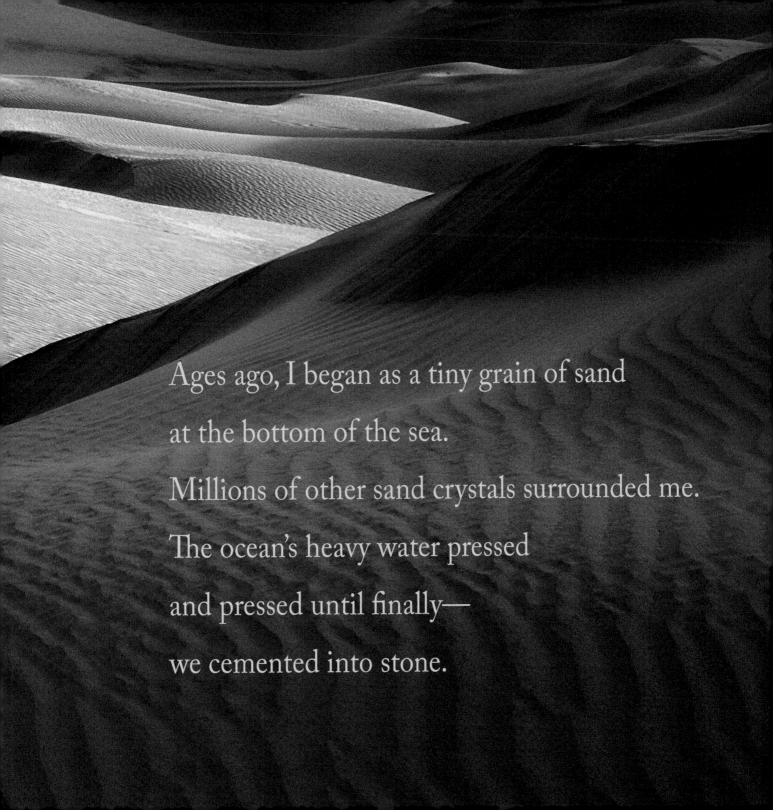

Ages ago, I began as a tiny grain of sand

at the bottom of the sea.

Millions of other sand crystals surrounded me.

The ocean's heavy water pressed

and pressed until finally—

we cemented into stone.

You began as one tiny cell, as small as a grain of sand.

From one cell, you became two,
then four.
Now you are made of millions
of connected cells.

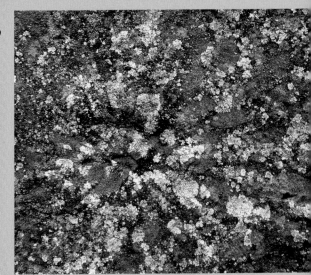

From one tiny cell, you became a person.

From one grain of sand, I became a mountain.

Change

does not stop.

Not for you,

not for me.

Rain pours down

my strong,

smooth

back.

Water trickles
through tiny
cracks.

Narrow streams
flash through
corkscrew
corridors,
slicing out
twisty, twirly,
skinny slot
canyons.

Wide rivers carve deep paths

and make giant canyons, mazes of canyons,

and one of the world's biggest, the Grand Canyon.

Howling winds loosen sand

and blow it, pile it, into soft, sloping dunes.

Climb up, up, up on top of me,

and slide down,

down,

down!

Seasons of wind and rain

wear away my cliffs and walls.

Soon my old sides sag.

Stone crumbles back to sand,

washes into creeks,

rushes down arroyos.

Big boulders tumble.

Boom!

Crash!

Slabs of stone

slide off cliffs,

change walls

into caves,

alcoves, or

arches.

Sometimes my crusty, hard-topped layers stay,

while underneath soft layers change.

I become a sandstone goblin,

a hoodoo, or a candy-cane column,

giant elephant toes...

See my wide-brimmed Mexican hat?

Sometimes change happens where no one can see—
almost invisibly.

Rivers disappear underground
and flow between rocky layers.

Mineral
jackets wrap
around each
sand crystal
and create
walls of color,
ribbons and
waves of
color.

Sometimes I change like magic.

Sandstone walls glow as if on fire.

Puddles fill with turquoise sky, reflect and tease.

Sand, rocks, and stone keep changing,

sometimes fast, sometimes very slow—

Just like you!

Glossary

Ancient Ones People who lived hundreds and hundreds of years ago in the American Southwest. They are sometimes called Anasazi. They built homes called pueblos, made pottery, and painted or carved rock art on cliffs or in caves. They also left behind their handprints. Their relatives, the Hopi, Zuni, and other pueblo tribes, still live on the high mesas of Arizona and New Mexico.

Arroyo A stream or creek that gushes full of water after a summer rain, but sits dry and dusty between rain showers.

Candy-Cane Column Layers of red and pink sand, or sediment, that are pressed together to make stone, then worn away to form tall rock towers with stripes that look like candy canes. Sometimes volcanic ash forms dark stripes.

Canyon Over a long period of time, wind and water can cut through a mountain of rock to make a long, deep hole called a canyon. It just takes a million years or so.

Crystal Crystals are beautiful, sparkling rocks. They are formed when teeny tiny particles, called atoms, which are too small for the human eye to see, come together in a certain pattern over time. Crystals have very smooth surfaces that are called faces, just like your face.

Earthquake Our planet is made up of huge plates of earth that fit together kind of like a jigsaw puzzle. These plates move around really slowly. When the plates hit one another along their edges, they can cause an earthquake, which makes the ground shake for a little while. The shaking spreads out from the edges of the plates, just like ripples spread out when you drop a pebble into a pond.

Grand Canyon The Grand Canyon is in northern Arizona and is one of the largest canyons in the world. It is more than a mile deep and 277 miles long, and it averages ten miles from rim to rim! It was formed when water cut through red, pink, yellow, and even purple sandstone. When you look into the Grand Canyon, you are looking back in time. The oldest rocks you can see at the bottom are about 2 billion years old.

Hoodoo, Goblin, Mushroom, and Capped Column

Colored layers of sandstone, each a different hardness, are lifted, shifted, and twisted over time. Water and wind wear away the softer layers underneath faster than the harder layers on top. This forms weird shapes. Some look like elephant toes or Mexican hats; others look like mushrooms or scary goblins.

Mineral Minerals are found in the earth. They are made up of elements such as oxygen and iron. Minerals combine to create all the different types of rocks, including sandstone, a sedimentary rock.

Monument Valley In Monument Valley, along the northern edge of Arizona and the southern edge of Utah, wind has carved rocks into giant statues, also called monuments. Two of them look like giant mittens. Monument Valley is a special place for the Navajo people.

Plateau, Mesa, Butte, Chimney, Spire Water and wind can also cut into sedimentary rocks and leave large, flat mountains that look like the top of a table. When the sides of the table are steep, or straight, and the top is big, it is called a plateau or a mesa. If more wind and water whittle away at the sides, it leaves a smaller block on top, and then the table is called a butte. Even more wind and water can make the butte even thinner, and then it is called a chimney or a spire.

Sandstone This type of rock is made when grains of sand are cemented, or glued, together over time. First water or wind gather the sand, then more water presses down on the sand, which glues it together into stone. Sandstone is like a sponge; there is space between the grains of sand, so it holds water very well. Sometimes you'll even see trees growing in sandstone, because water is able to get to their roots.

Sediment Tiny bits of rock, shells, and even volcanic ash are called sediment. You might call it sand. When sediment is pressed together, it becomes sedimentary rock.

Shale This type of sedimentary rock is made when tiny grains of clay are pressed together and all the water is squeezed out.

Slot Canyon Slot canyons start out as a crack in a wall of rock. Rushing water makes the crack bigger and deeper, until a slot canyon is formed. Slot canyons are usually skinny and twisty because of the way water winds through them and grinds away the rock.

Text © 2009 Nancy Bo Flood
Photographs © 2009 Tony Kuyper

Library of Congress Cataloging-in-Publication Data

Flood, Nancy Bo.
  Sand to stone : and back again / by Nancy Bo Flood ; photographs by Tony Kuyper.
    p. cm.
  ISBN 978-1-55591-657-2 (pbk.)
  1. Sandstone--Colorado Plateau--Juvenile literature. 2. Sandstone--Colorado Plateau--Pictorial works. I. Kuyper, Tony, ill. II. Title.
  QE471.15.S25F56 2009
  552'.5--dc22
                              2008052833

Printed in the United States
0 9 8 7 6 5 4 3 2

Design by Ann W. Douden

Fulcrum Publishing
4690 Table Mountain Drive, Suite 100
Golden, Colorado 80403
800-992-2908 • 303-277-1623
http://fulcrum.bookstore.ipgbook.com

Acknowledgments

To my first and finest editor, William Flood—always, thank you.

Vermont College faculty and fellow students, please stand and receive a round of applause, especially Ellen Howard, who repeated, "through line," until I got it.

Flagstaff plateau authors—Kay Jordan, Marty Crump, Steve Hirst, Martha Blue, and Marilyn Taylor, steady and solid as old buttes, my appreciation should be carved in stone.

Thank you to geologist David O'Leary for reviewing the text.

Special thanks to Faith Marcovecchio and Ann Douden for creating this amazing book from our images and words.